T3-BUV-193

Across
Five
Aprils

and Related Readings

McDougal Littell
A HOUGHTON MIFFLIN COMPANY

Evanston, Illinois   Boston   Dallas

ISBN 0-395-78367-4

234567—MAL—02 01 00 99 98 97 96

Table of Contents

Parts of the SourceBook 2

Overview Chart 3

Customizing Instruction 4

Into the Literature: *Creating Context*

Across Five Aprils 5

An Award-Winning Author 5

Why Do They Fight? 5

Hunt's Life 6

Hunt on Hunt 6

Literary Concept: Theme 7

Literary Concept: Character Development 8

Motivating Activities 9

Through the Literature: *Developing Understanding*

Across Five Aprils Discussion Starters 10–12

Related Readings Discussion Starters 13–18

from *The Boys' War* 13

"The Mysterious Mr. Lincoln," "The Gettysburg Address" 14

"The Drummer Boy of Shiloh" 15

"Around the Campfire," "The Huts at Esquimaux" 16

"The Sniper" 17

from *Voices from the Civil War* 18

Reproducible Pages for Students 19

FYI: *Across Five Aprils* 20–25

FYI: "The Mysterious Mr. Lincoln" 26

FYI: "The Drummer Boy of Shiloh" 27

FYI: "The Sniper" 28

FYI: Glossary 29–30

Strategic Reading 1–3 31–33

Literary Concept 1–2 34–35

Beyond the Literature: *Synthesizing Ideas*

Culminating Writing Assignments 36

Multimodal Activities 37–38

Cross-Curricular Projects 39–41

Suggestions for Assessment 42

Test 43

Test Answer Key 44–45

Additional Resources 46–48

Parts of the SourceBook

- **Table of Contents**
- **Overview Chart**
- **Customizing Instruction**

Into the Literature:
CREATING CONTEXT

- **Cultural/Historical/Author Background**
- **Literary Concepts**
- **Motivating Activities**

Through the Literature:
DEVELOPING UNDERSTANDING

- **Discussion Starters** Questions for the class to respond to orally after each section, including a Literary Concept question and a Writing Prompt
- (FYI) **FYI Pages for Students** Reproducible masters that offer students background, vocabulary help, and connections to the modern world as they read the literature
- (FYI) **Glossary** Reproducible glossary of difficult words for student use from each section of *Across Five Aprils*
- **Strategic Reading worksheets** Reproducible masters to help students keep track of the plot as they read (Literal and inferential reading)
- **Literary Concept worksheets** Reproducible masters to help students understand the use of literary elements such as theme (Critical reading)

Beyond the Literature:
SYNTHESIZING IDEAS

- **Culminating Writing Assignments** Exploratory, research, and literary analysis topics for writing, covering both the main work and the related readings
- **Multimodal Activities** Suggestions for short-term projects; some are cross-curricular.
- **Cross-Curricular Projects** Suggestions for long-term, cross-curricular, cooperative learning projects
- **Suggestions for Assessment**
- **Test, Answer Key** Essay and short-answer test on *Across Five Aprils* and related readings and answer key
- **Additional Resources** Additional readings for students (coded by difficulty level) and teachers, as well as bibliographic information about commercially available technology

Links to The Language of Literature:

Connections can easily be made between *Across Five Aprils* and **Unit 4, Facing the Enemy, Part 1, So Much at Stake** in *The Language of Literature,* Grade 8.

Literature Connections	SourceBook	Reproducible Pages
Across Five Aprils	Customizing Instruction, p. 4 Into the Literature: Creating Context, pp. 5–6 Literary Concepts: Theme, Character Development, pp. 7–8 Motivating Activities, p. 9	**FYI, pp. 20–21** **Glossary, pp. 29–30**
Across Five Aprils Section 1, pp. 1–47	Discussion Starters, p.10	**FYI, pp. 22–23** **Glossary, p. 29** **Strategic Reading 1, p. 31** **Literary Concept 1, p. 34**
Across Five Aprils Section 2, pp. 48–130	Discussion Starters, p. 11	**FYI, pp. 24** **Glossary, pp. 29–30** **Strategic Reading 2, p. 32** **Literary Concept 2, p. 35**
Across Five Aprils Section 3, pp. 131–213	Discussion Starters, p. 12	**FYI, p. 25** **Strategic Reading 3, p. 33** **Glossary, p. 30**
from *The Boys' War,* pp. 216–224	Discussion Starters, p. 13	
"The Mysterious Mr. Lincoln," pp. 225–229	Discussion Starters, p. 14	**FYI, p. 26**
"The Gettysburg Address," pp. 230–231	Discussion Starters, p. 14	**FYI, p. 26**
"The Drummer Boy of Shiloh," pp. 232–238	Discussion Starters, p. 15	**FYI, p. 27**
"Around the Campfire," pp. 239–240	Discussion Starters, p. 16	
"The Huts at Esquimaux," pp. 241–242	Discussion Starters, p. 16	
"The Sniper," pp. 243–248	Discussion Starters, p. 17	**FYI, p. 28**
from *Voices from the Civil War* pp. 249–252	Discussion Starters, p. 18	
	Culminating Writing Assignments, p. 36 Multimodal Activities, pp. 37–38 Cross-Curricular Projects, pp. 39–41 Suggestions for Assessment, p. 42 Test, Answer Key, pp. 43–45 Additional Resources, pp. 46–48	

Customizing Instruction

Less Proficient Readers

- Students may have difficulty with the use of dialect in this novel. Explain that dialect is a variation of a language spoken by the people of a region or a group. Ask if students know of any examples of dialect in their own experience.

- Tell students that dialect can vary from a language in three ways:

  1. in pronunciation: "Jenny is *fur and away* too young to be thinkin' about Shad *or ary* other young man" (In this example, *fur* is an altered pronunciation of *far* and *ary* is a variation on *any* and *nary.*)

  2. in grammar: "I guess you *heered* about Chickamauga."

  3. in vocabulary: "The Potomac boys are *mitey hifalutin.*"

- For students who continue to have trouble with comprehension, create small groups in which each student in turn reads and interprets the dialect and other difficult words in Chapter 1.

- Ask students to summarize the action at the end of each chapter.

- Some students may have trouble with literal comprehension of the events in the novel. Reproduce and have these students use **Strategic Reading 1–3** worksheets, pages 30–32, as they read to keep track of the plot development.

Students Acquiring English

- Use a map in class to illustrate the position of the states and territories. Bring in Civil War terms such as *Yankees, Confederacy,* and others, and show the flags of the Union and Confederacy.

- Show a videotape version of *Across Five Aprils.*

- Ask students from other countries to summarize the issues in civil wars in their nations' histories.

- Use the suggestions for Less Proficient Readers listed above.

Gifted and Talented Students

- Have students trace historical events in the FYI time line (page 20), adding the fictionalized events in the book to the time line.

- Have students identify and trace a theme of their choice through the book. You might want to list two or three examples such as *conflicting loyalties* or *courage* to help students get started.

- **Vocabulary** If you wish to teach vocabulary, 23 useful words on the **Glossary** pages have been asterisked. Suggest that students explore different parts of speech that derive from the same root:

Verb	Noun	Adjective/Adverb
emancipate	emancipator	emancipated

Into the Literature

CREATING CONTEXT

Across Five Aprils

Irene Hunt's *Across Five Aprils,* published in 1964, is a historical novel set at the time of the American Civil War. A historical novel is an imagined story set in the past with characters, setting, and action drawn from the records of actual events. The historical novelist blends fiction and nonfiction by inventing fictional characters to take part in the past—often in times of great cultural conflict, such as wars or political and social unrest.

Across Five Aprils is an excellent example of a historical novel. Its principal character is Jethro, a boy modeled after Hunt's grandfather, who, like Jethro, was nine when the Civil War began. Hunt includes details that show the war's devastating effects not only on the soldiers in the field but also on the everyday lives of people at home. Adapting historical records— newspaper articles and letters—she is careful to provide only information that would have been accessible to a rural family far from the lines of battle, making the events seem personal and immediate. As much as the story of a war, *Across Five Aprils* is a chronicle of a young boy's growing up. The war forces Jethro to confront the difficulties of choosing sides in situations that have no clear-cut resolutions as he struggles with the complexities of a troubled period in American history.

An Award-Winning Author

Across Five Aprils has won two of the most respected awards that a book for young people can receive. The first is the Charles W. Follett Award for worthy contributions to literature for young people; the winning author received a $3,000 cash prize and the gold Follett Award Medal. *Across Five Aprils* is also a Newbery Medal Honor Book, recognized by a committee of the American Library Committee. The Newbery Medal is named for the first publisher of children's periodicals. Irene Hunt's *Up a Road Slowly* (1966) also won a Newbery Award.

Why Do They Fight?

Those who study history often wonder why people are willing to risk their lives in battle. In the Civil War, the answer seems easier for the South: their homes and way of life were at stake. But why would others brave that deadly fire? Below are some answers from their letters.

"I will fight till I die if necessary for the liberties which you have so long enjoyed." (Missouri)

"I do feel that the liberty of the world is placed in our hands to defend, and if we are overcome then farewell to freedom." (Massachusetts)

"When there is no officer with us, we take no prisoners.... We want revenge for our brother soldiers and will have it...." (Wisconsin)

from McPherson, James M. *What They Fought For: 1861–1865.* Baton Rouge: Louisiana State University Press, 1994.

Hunt's Life

Irene Hunt was born on May 18, 1907, in Pontiac, Illinois. At six weeks of age, she moved to Newton, Illinois, the same area in which *Across Five Aprils* is set. When her father died in 1914, Hunt moved to her grandparents' farm, where she lived until she was twelve. It was there that she heard her grandfather's stories of the Civil War, but it would be years before she turned them into *Across Five Aprils*. She began teaching English and French in Oak Park, Illinois, taught psychology at the University of South Dakota, and returned to Cicero, Illinois, to teach elementary and junior high school.

In the early 1960s, while still teaching, Hunt began writing fiction. Her work bore fruit in 1964 when *Across Five Aprils* was published by Follett Publishing Co. The novel won the Charles M. Follett award in 1964 and was the sole runner-up for the Newbery Medal in 1965. Hunt's second novel, *Up a Road Slowly* (1966), fared even better. The story of a young girl's life after her mother dies, it won the Newbery Medal in 1967. With two successes to her credit, Hunt retired from teaching in 1969 to write full time.

Hunt now lives and works in St. Petersburg, Florida. In her spare time, she enjoys refinishing old furniture, painting, and traveling in France, but her chief interest remains children. Esther Meeks, a writer for the *Library Journal*, sums up Hunt's goals for children's literature: "[To] help children to understand themselves and other people, [to] help them not only to grow up but to grow." As Hunt herself puts it, "I believe I am one of those people who remember what it is like to be a child—the bewilderments and uncertainties as well as the joys."

Hunt on Hunt

On her own writing—

"Words have always held a fascination for me, causing me to be teased often as a child when I used them lavishly without having the slightest idea of their meaning. The wish to write pages full of words, to make them tell the stories that I dreamed about, haunted me from childhood on."

FROM *DICTIONARY OF LITERARY BIOGRAPHY*

On writing *Across Five Aprils*—

"I had a kindly, storytelling grandfather whose stories greatly influenced my writing. . . During the early sixties while teaching social studies to junior high school students, I felt that teaching history through literature was a happier, more effective process. . . Suddenly, I realized how [my grandfather's stories] might be put to use. My books were generated by the needs of my students."

QUOTED BY LEE HOPKINS IN *MORE BOOKS BY MORE PEOPLE*

On great books—

"Great books do not have to preach. But they do speak to the conscience, the imagination, and the heart of many a child. And they speak with very clear and forceful voices."

QUOTED IN *THE HORN BOOK MAGAZINE*, August 1967

Literary Concept
THEME

As a writer of historical fiction, Irene Hunt sets her stories in periods that interest her both as a writer and as a teacher. In her novels, she brings to distant historical events the feel of real life, in part by her treatment of her favorite **themes.** One such theme is the idea that untested beliefs often bring a person into conflict. In several novels, and especially in *Across Five Aprils,* Hunt shows us individuals, families, and whole sections of the country coming into conflict with each other because of their beliefs.

Across Five Aprils explores this and other themes related to it. Below are some of the themes that run through the novel.

- All people have beliefs, but beliefs that are unexamined can lead to pain, strife, and even war.
- Individual loyalties can conflict with the values and loyalties of a community.
- Most often there are no real winners in a war; both sides suffer.
- Some decisions are difficult to make because they are neither wrong nor right.
- Our lives are often affected by circumstances beyond our control.
- Hardship and challenges to one's beliefs offer opportunities for growth.
- Justice does not always proceed according to human timetables or individual ideas of right and wrong.

Presentation Suggestions Before students read the novel, remind them that the **theme** of a literary work is an insight about life or human nature that the writer presents to the reader. Then read one or two themes and ask students to give examples from real life that support those statements. Suggest that they look for ways events in the novel support those ideas also. Have them try to discover other themes that the novel suggests. When they finish the novel, have them work in pairs or in small groups to complete the **Literary Concept 1** worksheet, page 34, to think further about themes.

Literary Concept

CHARACTER DEVELOPMENT IN COMING-OF-AGE NOVELS

In many novels, the central character goes through a series of challenging and sometimes painful episodes as he or she grows up. Experiencing such events causes the central character to significantly change his or her understanding of and attitudes toward the world's complexities. Such changes are often reflected in the character's own words and actions, in the comments about the character made by the author as narrator, or by the other characters.

Jethro in *Across Five Aprils* is the character who undergoes the most significant changes in attitude and awareness. When we first see him, he is a young boy of nine, helping his mother with spring planting. He seems secure in his world and in his opinions about it. Very soon, however, Jethro is faced with events and situations that strike a series of blows to his own beliefs. Civil war comes and he sees that war is not so simple as he once thought. He learns that justice cannot be quickly and easily gained by exacting vengeance. He learns that war brings suffering to people in countless ways, and even then does not settle all the issues that caused it.

In short, Jethro, over the course of "five Aprils," is forced to grow up in ways he never anticipates and that he cannot control. He is more or less innocent when the novel opens. By its end, the experience of war has forced him to make difficult choices, thereby losing his innocence and assuming the responsibilities of an adult.

One reason authors write the coming-of-age novel is that most readers can easily identify with its dramatic conflicts. All humans must grow up, and to do so must change the ideas and beliefs they once had. Most of us must exchange simple, tidy, untested beliefs for more complex ideas about how life works. By emphasizing certain key experiences of testing ideas against reality, coming-of-age novels dramatize the changes all people go through as they mature.

Irene Hunt, in *Across Five Aprils,* goes further. In a sense, Jethro's growing up parallels the growth of the United States itself. Before the Civil War, many Americans lived in a state of innocence, holding, like Jethro, unexamined beliefs. During the Civil War, each side's views about being wholly in the right were severely tested. As in Jethro's family, brothers had to make choices that put them in mortal conflict with friends, families, and their own communities. The experiences of the Civil War thus made America, both North and South, a more complex and less innocent place than it had once been.

Presentation Suggestions Help students see the changes Jethro goes through in *Across Five Aprils.* Have them fill out the **Literary Concept 2** worksheet on page 35, **Character Development**, as they read the novel.

Motivating Activities

1. **Class Discussion** Ask students to imagine how their lives would change if our country had a civil war today. Suppose, for example, that their state were at war with two neighboring states. How would their lives be affected? Make a chart on the board and have students suggest ideas and list changes under such categories as Daily Life, Travel, Family Relations, Activities, Immediate Future.

2. **Role-Playing** Have students discuss or role-play one of the situations that follow:

   • A close friend has done something that your community sees as shameful. The wrongdoer asks for your help covering up or getting away. How do you respond? Will you help? To what lengths will you go in providing aid?

   • Imagine that you and a classmate have a serious disagreement. Other members of the class and your friends side with your classmate. Will the opinions of others make you change your mind? Will you try to convince others you are right? What else might you consider doing?

3. **Tapping Prior Knowledge: The Civil War** Invite students to work in small groups to share what they already know about the Civil War. Each group can take a different aspect of the war: the North's reasons for fighting, the South's reasons for fighting, the effect of the war on those at home and on the economies of the North and South, the outcome, its aftermath, and so on. Each group can chart its information and present it to the class as a whole. This information should be saved to help students work through the novel and its events.

4. **Linking to Today: Growing Up** Help students look into their experience and expectations about growing up. Begin by having students volunteer several different ways in which someone grows up—physically, intellectually, socially, morally. Then have them discuss the positives and negatives of growing up as they see it: they gain more freedom as they get older but more responsibility, more power but harder decisions, and so on. To make this more concrete, have students in small groups create evaluation diagrams: first elicit a set of criteria (e.g. "freedom"), number the criteria in order of importance, and decide whether each is a favorable, unfavorable, or neutral aspect of growth. To give students more perspective, encourage them to look backward in life as well as forward: is being twelve years old better than being six? Two? Does growing up end? If so, when? Conclude by having students look for the type of growth each character undergoes in *Across Five Aprils*.

5. **FYI Background** Reproduce and distribute to students the FYI pages (pages 20 and 21) that gives background information on the Civil War. You might reproduce and distribute all the FYI pages for the novel at this time for students to refer to as they read the novel.

BEFORE READING

You might want to distribute

 pp. 22–23, Glossary, p. 29

Across Five Aprils

SECTION 1

Chapters 1–3

AFTER READING

Discussion Starters

1. If you were Jethro, how would you feel at this point in the story?

2. How do Jethro's beliefs about the war change in this section?

3. Compare Bill's attitude about war with that of Wilse Graham and his brothers. Which do you agree with more? Why? What advice would you give Bill?

4. **Literary Concept: Foreshadowing** Some authors use foreshadowing, or clues that point to later events. What do you think Jethro's talk on Copernicus predicts about people, including Jethro himself, and their beliefs about the coming Civil War?

   CONSIDER

   ✓ how Copernicus's contemporaries reacted to his ideas

   ✓ how strongly people in 1861 believed in slavery or abolition

   ✓ how Jethro's mother reacts to Copernicus's name

5. Do you think people's attitudes toward engaging in war have changed since Jethro's day? In what ways?

Writing Prompt

Suppose that you are an editor for a Northern or Southern newspaper. Write an **editorial** responding to the news of the attack on Fort Sumter.

SECTION 2

Chapters 4—7

AFTER READING

Discussion Starters

1. Which character has impressed you the most so far? Describe the actions of the character whom you admire most and what qualities they seem to reveal.

2. What does the barn-burning incident teach Jethro about people, both good and bad?

3. At this point, what instances of justice do you see taking place in the story?

4. In describing Jethro's ride with Dave Burdow, the author says, "the world was turning upside down for Jethro." What does the narrator mean by this? How do later events prove the statement true?

5. Shadrach Yale says, "It took more courage for Bill to do what he did than it does for John and me to carry out our plans." What does he mean? Do you agree? Explain your answer.

6. Describe a time when you heard or read about someone's taking justice into his or her own hands the way Wortman and his allies do. Identify the issue that was at stake and evaluate the consequences of the act. Explain what you think should be done with the perpetrator.

Writing Prompt

When Jenny receives Shad's love letter, she refuses to share it with Jethro. Put yourself in Jethro or Jenny's place and write a **diary entry** describing your opinion and feelings about keeping Shad's letter private.

You might want to distribute

 p. 25, Glossary p. 30

SECTION 3

Chapter 8–12

AFTER READING

Discussion Starters

1. On the whole, did you like this novel? Why or why not?

2. The author says that the fifth April of her story was the "saddest and most cruel" of all. How would you describe it? Give examples to show what you mean.

3. Jethro's most difficult decision probably comes when he finds out Eb is a deserter. What made his decision difficult? Would you defend or disagree with his decision to break the law? Explain your answer.

4. Jethro, like many Americans during the Civil War, was "hungry for a hero." Does anyone qualify as a hero for Jethro in the end? For the American people? Explain why you think so.

5. **Literary Concept: Metaphor** A metaphor compares two unlike things without using the words "like" or "as." In describing Eb, the narrator says, "Then a skeleton came out from among the trees." What does the metaphor add to the scene here?

> ### CONSIDER
>
> ✓ what the metaphor suggests about Eb's condition
>
> ✓ what it suggests about Jethro's reaction to the sight of his cousin

Writing Prompt

Add an **afterword** to the book that tells what happened to Bill after the war. Did he return? Use your imagination.

from The Boys' War

Discussion Starters

1. What is your reaction to the hardships faced by the Civil War soldiers described in this article?

2. Which account of the soldiers' fear—Irene Hunt's novel or Jim Murphy's essay—do you find more compelling? Why?

3. Think about Civil War prisoners who went into business making jewelry or selling rats for food. What does this say about prison conditions? What does it say about human nature?

4. Many soldiers feared being wounded more than death itself. What details from *The Boy's War* and *Across Five April*s support that fear?

Writing Prompt

Suppose this article came out during the Civil War. Write a **letter to the editor** of the local newspaper telling why you think the article should or should not be published.

You might want to distribute

 p. 26

The Mysterious Mr. Lincoln

AFTER READING

Discussion Starters

1. How does the Lincoln of Russell Freedman's essay compare with the way Lincoln is portrayed in *Across Five Aprils*?

2. As Freedman points out, Lincoln did not begin the war to free the South's slaves. Should this affect his reputation as the Great Emancipator? Explain why or why not.

3. Freedman maintains that Lincoln was the most unpopular president the United States had ever had. Does this affect your opinion of Lincoln's worth? Why or why not?

4. What do you think about the contrast between a person's public face and his or her "real" face? Is it desirable, or possible, for a person to be the same in public and in private? Explain.

Writing Prompt

If you were Lincoln, how would you respond to some of the statements of criticism mentioned in this article? Write a short **defense** of yourself.

The Gettysburg Address

AFTER READING

Discussion Starters

1. What is your impression of the Gettysburg Address? Do you think it still deserves its famous reputation? Support your opinion with reasons.

2. In *Across Five Aprils,* Jethro's mother says, "It has the ring of Scriptures about it." What does she mean? What sounds "Scriptural"—either in language or meaning—in Lincoln's speech?

3. Lincoln never names the two great issues of the war—preserving the Union and ending slavery—yet they are clearly implied in his speech. What words or phrases refer to these two issues? Be specific.

Writing Prompt

Many people criticized Lincoln's speech when they heard it or read it. Suppose you are a Confederate. Write a **criticism** of this speech, analyzing its weaknesses in language and ideas from a Confederate point of view.

You might want to distribute

 p. 27

The Drummer Boy of Shiloh

Discussion Starters

1. In *Across Five Aprils*, you read about some Civil War battles. What does "The Drummer Boy of Shiloh" add to your sense of what such a battle might be like?

2. The story begins with Joby feeling so helpless and afraid that he cries. What are his feelings at the end? What has changed?

3. Evaluate this General who admits he has been crying like a boy. Explain your opinion.

4. The General tells Joby that the drummer is almost as important as the "general of the army." In what sense is this true?

5. In several places, the author uses falling peach blossoms as a metaphor. What does the image of falling peach blossoms suggest about the coming battle? What other associations do you have with this image?

Writing Prompt

Write an **epilogue** to Ray Bradbury's story by having the drummer boy, now an old man, describe the next day's battle. Include what happens to the General.

Around the Campfire
The Huts at Esquimaux

Discussion Starters

1. What is the overall sense of war you get from "Around the Campfire"? How does it compare to the understanding you got from *Across Five Aprils*?

   CONSIDER

   ✓ the initial idea of young men that the war would be a "picnic"
   ✓ their attitude once they had been in battle

2. How would you explain the speaker's contrast between the value of the first two episodes in "Around the Campfire" and his last statement, "From this, I didn't learn a thing." Why do you think the wounding of his friend is said to be "useless"?

3. Think about the mood of the speaker in "The Huts at Esquimaux." Which line or image in the poem do you think conveys his mental state best? Explain.

4. When the speaker in "The Huts at Esquimaux" talks about shooting a Rebel, what is his tone? He may have more than one attitude. Explain.

5. Restate in your own words what the speaker in "The Huts at Esquimaux" is conveying about his experience in the Civil War. Compare or contrast it to the effects of being exposed to acts of violence on TV.

6. Which characters in *Across Five Aprils* would probably most agree with each poem? Explain your choices.

Writing Prompt

Write a **dialogue** between the Texas boy in "Around the Campfire" and the speaker in "The Huts at Esquimaux" on what war does to a person.

You might want to distribute

 p. 28

The Sniper

AFTER READING

Discussion Starters

1. What was your reaction to the end of the story? Explain.

2. With whom do you think the narrator's sympathies lie in this story?

> ### CONSIDER
>
> ✓ the description of the sniper's killing the old woman
>
> ✓ the description of his being wounded
>
> ✓ the description of his killing his opponent
>
> ✓ the description of his recognizing his opponent

3. This story puts very concisely what the narrator considers the greatest danger in civil war. Do you agree? Disagree? Explain your answer.

4. What do you think is the theme, or message, of this story? Considering Bill's last words to his brother in *Across Five Aprils,* do you think Bill would agree with it? Explain.

5. **Literary Concept: Irony** Irony is a contrast between what is expected and what actually exists or happens. What is ironic about the ending of "The Sniper"?

Writing Prompt

Write an interior **monologue** of what goes through the sniper's mind minutes after he discovers he has shot his brother.

from Voices from the Civil War

Discussion Starters

1. Which of these selections is most powerful to you? Why?
2. After reading all three selections, what do you think about soldiers who desert their comrades in battle? Give your reasons.
3. The selections give very different solutions to the problem of desertion. Review and identify the solutions. How is each of these reflected in *Across Five Aprils?*
4. In the first selection, the writer refers to "the physical fear of going forward and the moral fear of turning back." What is the difference between the two? Which fear do you think is more powerful?

Writing Prompt

Considering what Abraham Lincoln wrote to Jethro, write a **reply** from the President to any one of these writers.

REPRODUCIBLE PAGES **FYI** **for STUDENTS to USE INDEPENDENTLY**

These pages for the students give background, explain references, provide help with vocabulary words, and help students connect the modern world with the world of *Across Five Aprils.* You can reproduce them and allow students to read them before or while they are reading the works in the Literature Connections

Table of Contents

Background 20–21

Section 1: Chapters 1–3 22–23

Section 2: Chapters 4–7 24

Section 3: Chapters 8–12 25

The Mysterious Mr. Lincoln 26

The Drummer Boy of Shiloh 27

The Sniper 28

Glossary 29–30

Across Five Aprils

THE NORTH
United States of America

President:
Abraham Lincoln

Leading Generals:
Ulysses S. Grant
William T. Sherman

Goals:
Preservation of the Union
Increased modernization
and industrialization
End of slavery

Abraham Lincoln
16th President of the U.S.
1809–1865

The Civil War: Some Facts

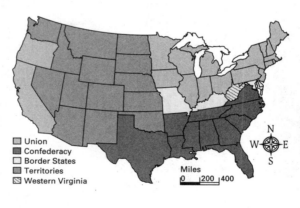

☐ Union
■ Confederacy
☐ Border States
■ Territories
▨ Western Virginia

Miles
0   200   400

N
W ⊕ E
S

THE SOUTH
Confederate States of America

President:
Jefferson Davis

Leading Generals:
Robert E. Lee
Stonewall Jackson

Goals:
Preservation of an
agricultural way of life
Preservation of slavery

Jefferson Davis
President of Confederate States
1808–1889

1861
• Confederate States of America are formed (1860–1861)
• Confederates attack Fort Sumter (April 12, 1861) — the Civil War begins

1863
• Lincoln's Emancipation Proclamation takes effect (January 1863)
• Confederate invasion of Pennsylvania stopped at Gettysburg by George Meade (July 1863)

• Battles at Chickamauga and Chattanooga September and November 1863)

• Lincoln's Gettysburg Address given at dedication to cemetery at Gettysburg, Pennsylvania (November 1863)

1865
• Confederate States of America formally surrender at Appomattox (April 9, 1865)
• President Lincoln assassinated (April 14,1865)
• Civil War ends (May 26, 1865)

1862
• General Ulysses S. Grant wins first major victory, at Fort Donelson
• Battle of Shiloh (April 1862)
• Confederate victories at second Battle of Bull Run and Fredericksburg (August and December 1862)

1864
• President Lincoln re-elected President of the U.S.
• General Sherman's March to the Sea, during which he defeats Confederate army at Atlanta, and occupies Savannah, Georgia (July–September 1864)
• Battle of Nashville (December 1864)

Across Five Aprils

"Butternuts"

Across Five Aprils is set in southern Illinois, beginning in 1861, a time when the region was still sparsely settled farm country. Illinois had been a state only since 1818. Although new railroads in the 1850s were making Chicago a major hub, the southern part of the state remained rural. Its people were known as *Butternuts* because of the oil from the butternut tree they used to dye their homespun clothes. Both Lincoln and Ulysses S. Grant came from Illinois, so most of the state supported the Union. In butternut areas, however, Union support was so weak that some talked of creating a separate state. Support for freed slaves was even weaker. In 1853, Illinois joined its neighbors, Ohio and Indiana, in passing an exclusion law that forbade African Americans from entering its borders. The divisions in Illinois reflected those in the nation at large.

Life on the Battlefield

Early in the war, soldiers were outfitted with muskets, smoothbore shoulder arms that were fitted with bayonets. Soon after, the development of the "minie," a bullet that traveled further than previous types, made bayonets useless.

The Confederate and Union armies used the same color codes: white or light blue for the infantry, scarlet for the artillery, and yellow for the cavalry. The soldiers' uniforms were sometimes dangerously similar: the outcome of a battle at Bull Run was determined when an officer misidentified a regiment's uniforms.

During winter months, soldiers built log cabins on the battlefield. They gave their homes names like Buzzard's Roost, Swine Hotel, Hole in the Wall, or Devil's Inn.

All the Comforts of Home

- For light, soldiers planted their rifle butts into the ground and stuck candles onto the bayonets.
- For stools, they used stumps or shipping crates.
- For tables, they used ammunition chests
- For bedding, they lay their blanket rolls out on bunks padded with pine needles, straw, and leaves.

Ulysses S. Grant, General and President, 1822—1885

Tom and Eb fought under Ulysses Simpson Grant at the battle of Fort Donelson in Tennessee; like Irene Hunt's fictional characters, Grant was the son of farmers. He graduated from the military academy at West Point, served in the Mexican War, then resigned his commission. When the Civil War broke out, Grant reenlisted, and, despite his heavy drinking, rose rapidly to the rank of Brigadier General. Grant proved to have a gift for leadership—his combination of daring, tenacity, and ruthlessness toward even his own men made his army almost unbeatable. However, Grant was much less effective in his two terms as President. His deathbed autobiography, *Personal Memoirs*, is considered a masterpiece of military history.

Chapters 1—3

LITERARY CONCEPT
Foreshadowing

Foreshadowing is a writer's use of hints or clues to indicate events that will occur later in the story. Jethro's talk about Copernicus foreshadows the effect the Civil War will have on the characters in *Across Five Aprils.* Similarly, his observation about Jenny's feelings about Shadrach's temporary departure draws our attention to the young couple in particular.

Chapter 1
Copernicus

Nicolaus Copernicus (1473–1543) is the "old feller" Jethro says gave people what they deserved—their "comeuppance." The founder of modern astronomy, Copernicus observed that the earth was not fixed, but moved. Like all the planets, it revolved around the sun, and completed a rotation on its axis once a day. His great book, *On the Revolutions of the Heavenly Spheres* (1543), explained this and other ideas. Copernicus had no equipment to prove his theories, but later astronomers, such as Galileo Galilei (1564–1642) and Johannes Kepler (1571–1630), soon did.

Chapter 2
Two Kinds of Slavery

When Wilse Graham speaks of "another evil in the name of industrialism," he is referring to what many called "wage slavery." Before the growth of industry between 1815 and 1860, most Americans had worked either as farmers or as craftsmen such as carpenters or seamstresses. Most worked for themselves, at their own pace. With the new factories came wage labor: workers did simple, repetitive jobs, worked long hours, and were easily replaced. To many, such labor was no better than slave labor. The boss hired and fired, and controlled one's hours and pay. Some even said that the American form of government required independent workers and so could not survive wage labor. And, like Wilse, Southerners argued that the North, with its own industrial "slavery," had no right to criticize the South.

The Soldier's Life

Most young farmers who volunteered to fight imagined rushing right into a battle that would be over quickly. Instead, they found themselves spending long, boring hours in camp. To occupy themselves, soldiers played games of all kinds. Some gambled at cards or dice. Others bet on horse races run by officers, or on cock fights. Some even had paper-boat races on nearby rivers. A favorite pastime, which the war helped spread nationwide, was the fairly new game of baseball. Even when equipment was unavailable, a game could be played with a yarn-wrapped walnut for a ball and a barrel stave for a bat.

April 12, 1861

Early in 1861, the seven Confederate States of America claimed possession of all forts and arsenals within Confederate territory—including Fort Sumter, located on Sullivan Island, at the entrance to Charleston Harbor in South Carolina. Shortly after taking office as president, Abraham Lincoln sent a relief expedition to Fort Sumter to support Major Robert Anderson, the Union commander there. The supplies did not arrive in time, however, and on April 12, Confederate General P.G.T. Beauregard shelled the fort, which surrendered the following day. Lincoln responded with a call for volunteers. The Civil War had begun.

VOCABULARY

Chapters 1, 2, 3
A Farmer's Dialect

Though dialects—regional varieties of Standard English— differ only in pronunciation, some dialect words have special meanings:

diggins	a place to live
tol'able	tolerable; not bad
allowed	figured, imagined
ary	any
mite	little, somewhat
spell	rest
what-fer	a beating
tykes	little children
holler	hollow

Chapter 3
Rural Schooling

Jethro was lucky to have a local school to go to. At the time of *Across Five Aprils,* the public school system was just beginning. As the teacher for the local common school, Shadrach Yale's salary would have been paid by the parents of his students or by taxes collected from the entire community. In some cases, people grumbled about the school tax. Others felt that parents should have full control over what their children learned. They didn't like the way that "common," or public, schools did not emphasize the Bible and its teaching.

Chapters 4—7

LITERARY CONCEPT

Allusion

An allusion is a reference to a historical or literary person, place, or event. In Chapter 4, Jethro expresses his doubts about Jenny marrying Shadrach before Shadrach leaves for the war. Shadrach replies, "Thou too, Brutus," an allusion to Brutus's betrayal of his friend Caesar in Shakespeare's play *Julius Caesar* (Act Three, Scene 2).

Chapter 5

Coffee Blues

Jethro's mother was not the only person who suffered from lack of coffee. In the South, due to the Union blockade, coffee nearly disappeared. If any could be found, it cost as much as 70 cents a pound. Coffee substitutes were made from okra seeds, toasted yams, and corn. By 1865, the shortages had worsened. In Petersburg, Virginia, that year, bacon and butter cost 20 cents a pound, while chickens cost 50 cents each.

Chapter 7
LITERARY CONCEPT

Irony

When Dan Lawrence tells the Creightons of Tom's death at Shiloh, he makes clear the irony of the situation—the contrast between what he expects and what actually happens. Tom has survived a day of horrible fighting. With the arrival of General Buell's reinforcements, Dan and Tom "waved and laughed like we was crazy." It is then, at his moment of greatest joy and relief, that Tom is struck dead. As you read, look for other ironic situations like this one.

Chapter 6

Copperheads

Copperheads was the name given to Northerners who sympathized with the South. It apparently was invented in the fall of 1861 when Ohio Republicans compared their Democratic opponents to the poisonous snakes known as copperheads. By 1862, the term was in use all over the country.

But Democrats refused to be insulted. They began to wear pins that showed the picture of Liberty that could be found on the copper penny in use at the time. The symbol was especially popular among the "Peace Democrats" who wanted to negotiate reunion with the South rather than fight a war.

The Peace Democrats' candidate for President in 1864 was General McClellan, who ran against Republican President Lincoln. He was against taking property from Southerners or forcing them to abolish slavery.

Chapters 8—12

VOCABULARY The military, like any specialized group, has its own vocabulary. The following is a glossary of military terms and Civil War slang.

When Soldiers Speak

vindictiveness	spite; vengefulness
clemency	mercy; an act of leniency
amnesty	general pardon
skirmish	a minor encounter in war
demote	to reduce to a lower rank or grade
post	an assigned station or task
maneuver	to guide with adroitness or design
secesh	Confederate, that is, "Secessionist," soldier

Chapter 8
Rifled Muskets

The "appalling slaughter" in the Civil War had several causes, but one of the most important was the new rifle used by foot soldiers. The old single-shot, smoothbore musket could fire accurately up to 80 yards. However, if gunmakers "rifled" the barrel—by making spiral grooves in it—the gun was accurate at 320 yards! In the 1850s, new, safer "minie" bullets made such rifles easy to use in battle.

Civil War commanders were slow to adapt to the new technology. With the old musket, tightly packed columns of troops could advance and fire together, safely outside musket range. Then at 80 yards they charged, using their bayonets before the defenders had time to re-load and fire. Against rifles, however, troops in tight formations hardly got to charge; most were picked off from a distance. At battles from Shiloh to Gettysburg, this is exactly what happened, and the slaughter was appalling.

Chapter 9
Deserters Came in Droves

As the war became ever crueler, soldiers deserted in ever greater numbers. Many things contributed to their decision. For some, it was seeing the wealthy pay for substitutes; in the South, plantation owners with 20 or more slaves were exempt from service. Still other soldiers could not ignore letters from their families, begging them to come home. Whatever the reasons, hundreds of thousands deserted. Though they could be shot, or branded with a *C* as cowards, one of every ten Union soldiers deserted; one of every seven Confederates did the same.

Chapter 10
Lincoln's Letter

The letter Jethro receives from President Lincoln is delivered to the town of Hidalgo, and Ed Turner brings it out to Jethro's house. Rural free delivery to homes far out in the countryside like the Creightons' wasn't fully established until 1896. In town things were much better. Starting in 1858, large communities had postal boxes that letters could be dropped into for collection. From 1845 to 1863, the cost of stamps and delivery depended on how far the letter had to travel across the country. But in 1863, one single rate was established.

The Mysterious Mr. Lincoln

BY RUSSELL FREEDMAN

Background

Though it might seem too "story-book" for Lincoln to write to a 10-year-old boy, it wasn't. Lincoln was a man of the people. Each morning he opened his White House door to any visitor who chose to come. He often told jokes to make people relax, and asked how he could help them. His staff warned that he was wearing himself out, but the President would not stop. He valued the "public opinion baths" that put him in touch with average Americans.

The President also reviewed all military courts-martial, seeking excuses to pardon the convicted. He called desertion cases his "leg cases," because of what he always said: "Almighty God gives a man a cowardly pair of legs, how can he help their running away with him?"

Abe the Widowmaker

While most people consider him one of the two greatest Presidents in American history, Abraham Lincoln was called less flattering names when he was alive. Especially in the election of 1864, Democrats lashed him for his Emancipation Proclamation and his continuance of the war. Among the vicious names applied to him were: "Abraham Africanus the First"; "brutal"; "obscene"; "an animal"; and "Abe the Widowmaker."

VOCABULARY

Chapter 11
The War of Words

deluded	deceived; misled
degradation	decline; a weakening
detractors	those who belittle or devalue
invective	an abusive or insulting expression
folly	lack of good sense; foolishness

... And the President Spoke, Too ...

At the Gettysburg dedication, it was Edward Everett, not the President, who was the featured speaker. Everett, the most renowned speaker in America, spoke for two hours, boring many. Then Lincoln took the podium, his Gettysburg Address written on lined paper, much of it composed on the train, the last words added at breakfast. The President spoke for only two minutes; he was done before a photographer could even take his picture. Few in the crowd applauded. Some newspapers left him out of their stories entirely. No wonder the President considered his speech a failure.

The Drummer Boy of Shiloh

BY RAY BRADBURY

Background

Civil War battles often had two names. The North tended to name battles after a nearby landmark—often a stream, like Bull Run. The South named battles after nearby towns, like Manassas. The exception was Shiloh. The North called it Pittsburgh Landing, after the river landing they defended, while the South named it for the little church nearby. The Southern name has stuck, perhaps because of the irony of the word *shiloh*: in Hebrew, it means "place of peace."

Talking Drums

In the confusion and noise of battle, soldiers needed a better form of communication than shouted commands. Drums served this purpose. Different beats signaled different moves in battle, and troops sighted on the drummer to keep their bearings. In camp, drums signaled such events as wake-up calls, formations, and meals. And when they weren't drumming, drummer boys did chores, cooked for the soldiers, and helped carry the wounded from the field.

An Easy Target

The importance of the drummer in battle had its disadvantage: drummers were a favorite target of enemy sharpshooters. Like other troops, drummers soon got used to being fired on, and even to being hit. One 14-year-old at the Battle of Vicksburg was hit several times by Confederate bullets, but kept on drumming. For his bravery, the drummer boy, Orion Howe, later got the Congressional Medal of Honor. He was lucky; hundreds were killed and thousands wounded before the war was over.

Johnny Shiloh

Sometimes the wounded piled up so quickly that drummer boys grabbed a spare rifle and began fighting. Johnny Clem, who did this at Shiloh, had joined a Michigan Regiment at age 11. In a few months he was drumming at the Battle of Shiloh. Cannon shells destroyed first one drum and then another. Clem then picked up a musket and started firing. The troops nicknamed him "Johnny Shiloh." Johnny Shiloh kept firing so well that he was made a sergeant in 1863—at the age of 13!

The Last Drummers

The Civil War would be the last war to use drummers in battle. Bigger, faster, and louder weapons made drumbeats ever harder to hear; bugles could cut through the noise better. Close formations and the slow advance had become a thing of the past. So had the drummer boys.

The Sniper

BY LIAM O'FLAHERTY

Background

Written in 1926, Liam O'Flaherty's story "The Sniper" was inspired by turbulent events in Ireland in the first quarter of the 20th century. In the late 1800s, many Irish people demanded greater independence from Great Britain, which had exercised control over Ireland from the beginning of the 19th century. Through the first quarter of this century, the Irish who opposed Great Britain's rule organized themselves into different parties and organizations. Some groups wanted complete independence from Great Britain. Other, more moderate groups were willing to compromise by sharing control over Ireland with the British government. Though Great Britain was seen as the common enemy, conflicts arose between many of the different Irish nationalist groups. In 1916, a failed Irish uprising took place that became known as the Easter Rebellion. Six years later, in 1922, tensions between two major groups erupted into civil war. For 18 months Ireland was torn by guerrilla warfare, sniper fire, and skirmishes that often pitted brother against brother. This civil war, effects of which are still felt to this day, ended in 1923.

VOCABULARY		
The Enemy Within	beleaguered	hemmed in; besieged
	spasmodically	proceeding in spasms; jerkily
	ascetic	one who is self-denying or austere
	fanatic	madly attached to a cause
	recoil	the kickback of a gun when fired
	gibber	to speak rapidly without making sense

Modern Day Ireland

Even though the Irish Civil War finally came to an end in 1923, fighting broke out again in the 1960s and continues to this day. Inspired by the Civil Rights movement in the United States, Catholics in Northern Ireland began protesting discrimination against them and demanding equality in the workplace and in the government. Their demands sparked angry reactions from Protestants, who argued that their control of industry and government was fair and democratic. After all, they were the majority. When tensions flared and violent figting began again in the late 1960s, the Irish Catholics' chief political party, Sinn Féin reacted by rearming its military. It is called the IRA, which stands for the Irish Republican Army.

Over the years, the IRA has carried out several terrorist attacks, killing Protestant police and politicians and bombing public restaurants and stores in England and Northern Ireland. The militant Protestants have retaliated by calling in the British army and letting Great Britain have more control over Northern Ireland. Finally in 1994, Catholics and Protestants reached a truce and began discussions working toward an independent Northern Ireland with a freely elected government and no British control.

Sinn Who?

English is not a native Irish language. The British brought it over when they invaded in the seventeenth century. As part of their effort to unify the country under its control, Great Britain banned Gaelic—Ireland's original tongue. Many Irish kept the language alive by speaking it and reading it in secret. Speaking it became an act of defiance during the Irish Rebellion and an expression of patriotism once southern Ireland won its independence. The tradition continues to this day. *Sinn Féin* is Gaelic for "We Ourselves."

Glossary

Section 1: Chapters 1–3

alleged (ə-lĕjd′): *adj.* supposed; so-called *p. 14*

arrogant* (ăr′ə-gənt): *adj.* self-important; haughty *p. 28*

authoritative* (ə-thôr′ĭ-tā′tĭv): *adj.* official; having an air of authority *p. 32*

buoyancy* (boi′ən-sē): *n.* gaiety; cheerfulness *p. 23*

emancipator* (ĭ-măn′sə-pā′tər): *n.* one who frees another *p. 39*

fiasco (fē-ăs′kō): *n.* complete failure *p. 38*

furor* (fyo͝or′ôr′): *n.* angry fit; rage *p. 11*

hypocrite* (hĭp′ə-krĭt′): *n.* one who professes beliefs, feelings, or virtues he or she does not hold *p. 32*

imminence (ĭm′ə-nəns): *n.* the quality of being about to happen *p. 8*

inevitably (ĭn-ĕv′ĭ-tə-blē): *adv.* unavoidably *p. 27*

melancholy* (mĕl′ən-kôl′ē): *adj.* gloomy; depressed *p. 8*

monotony* (mə-nŏt′n-ē): *n.* tiresome sameness *p. 24*

oratory (ôr′ə-tôr′ē): *n.* public speaking *p. 37*

somber* (sŏm′bər): *adj.* gloomy; dark in mood *p. 8*

strident (strīd′nt): *adj.* harsh *p. 35*

sullen* (sŭl′ən): *adj.* unsociably silent; resentful *p. 14*

tedium (tē′dē-əm): *n.* dullness; boredom *p. 37*

Section 2: Chapters 4–7

admonition* (ăd′mə-nĭsh′ən): *n.* a gentle warning *p. 54*

balefully (bāl′fəl-ē): *adv.* menacingly; malignantly *p. 64*

bluster* (blŭs′tər): *v.* to talk with noisy, often empty threats *p. 129*

immunity (ĭ-myo͞o′nĭ-tē): *n.* exemption from; a condition of being able to resist disease or other contagion *p. 127*

inept* (ĭn-ĕpt′): *adj.* incompetent; bungling *p. 127*

integrity* (ĭn-tĕg′rĭ-tē): *n.* complete sincerity or honesty *p. 121*

loathing (lō′thĭng): *n.* a feeling of disgust *p. 79*

mimicry (mĭm′ĭ-krē): *n.* the art or practice of imitating, or of copying to make fun of *p. 64*

niche (nĭch): *n.* a hollow space in a wall; a safe, suitable place *p. 126*

pompous* (pŏm′pəs): *adj.* overly showy or dignified *p. 64*

prestige (prĕ-stēzh′): *n.* influence; good reputation *p. 129*

scuttling (skŭt′lĭng): *adj.* scurrying; hurriedly withdrawing *p. 121*

shun* (shŭn): *v.* to deliberately avoid *p. 77*

tacit* (tăs′ĭt): *adj.* not spoken; implied by or inferred from *p. 94*

zeal (zēl): *n.* great eagerness for a cause *p. 121*

PARTIAL PRONUNCIATION KEY

ă	at, gas	îr	dear, here	th	thing, with
ā	ape, day	ng	sing, anger	*th*	then, other
ä	father, barn	ŏ	odd, not	ŭ	up, nut
âr	fair, dare	ō	open, road, grow	ûr	fur, earn, bird, worm
ĕ	egg, ten	ô	awful, bought, horse	zh	treasure, garage
ē	evil, see, meal	oi	coin, boy	ə	awake, even, pencil,
hw	white, everywhere	o͝o	look, full		pilot, focus
ĭ	inch, fit	o͞o	root, glue, through	ər	perform, letter
ī	idle, my, tried	ou	out, cow		

SOUNDS IN FOREIGN WORDS

kh	*German* ich, auch; *Scottish* loch	œ	*French* feu, cœur; *German* schön	ü	*French* utile, rue; *German* grün
n	*French* entre, bon, fin				

*The words followed by asterisks are useful words that you might add to your vocabulary.

Glossary (continued)

Section 3: Chapters 8–12

assuage (ə-swāj′): *v.* to ease; to pacify *p. 210*

atrocity* (ə-trŏs′ĭ-tē): *n.* a brutal or cruel deed *p. 199*

bigot (bĭg′ət): *n.* one intolerantly devoted to his or her own beliefs *p. 203*

complicity (kəm-plĭs′ĭ-tē): *n.* participation in something as if in guilt *p. 181*

contagion (kən-tā′jən): *n.* the transmission of a disease *p. 138*

convulsive (kən-vŭl′sĭv): *adj.* marked by violent, sudden movements *p. 153*

credence* (krēd′ns): *n.* acceptance; belief *p. 149*

delirium (dĭ-lîr′ē-əm): *n.* mental delusion of someone with high fever or injury *p. 171*

foray (fôr′ā′): *n.* a raid in search of spoils *p. 142*

forfeiture (fôr′fĭ-chŏŏr′): *n.* loss of some right or property due to an offense *p. 163*

gangrenous (găng′grə-nəs): *adj.* marked by death of cells from loss of blood, usually treated by amputation *p. 143*

incoherent (ĭn′kō-hîr′ənt): *adj.* loose; without order and clarity *p. 169*

plundering (plŭn′dər-ĭng): *n.* a taking of goods by force *p. 199*

presumption* (prĭ-zŭmp′shən): *n.* arrogance *p. 166*

reiterate* (rē-ĭt′ə-rāt′): *v.* to say or do over again; repeat *p. 161*

revile (rĭ-vīl′): *v.* to abuse with words; scold *p. 137*

rhetorically* (rĭ-tôr′ĭ-kəl-ē): *adv.* not intended to get an answer, for the answer is implied in the question *p. 188*

ruthlessness (rōōth′lĭs-nĭs): *n.* a lack of mercy or pity *p. 169*

siege (sēj): *n.* the surrounding of a place in order to force it to surrender *p. 189*

tenacity* (tə-năs′i-tē): *n.* determination; persistence *p. 138*

Name _____

Identifying Viewpoints

Jethro Creighton is the central character in *Across Five Aprils*. All other characters revolve around Jethro: Some instruct him, some serve as models for him, some puzzle him, some anger him, some cause him grief. Below is a chart showing the major people in Jethro's life. Indicate the following in the box provided:

- how each is related to Jethro
- each one's view of the coming war
- how Jethro perceives that character

If you can find a quote revealing that person's view of the war in Chapters 1–3, use that for the second column.

Character	Relation to Jethro	Character's View of War	How Jethro Perceives Character
1. Ellen Creighton			
2. Matt Creighton			
3. Bill Creighton			
4. John Creighton			
5. Wilse Graham			
6. Shadrach Yale			
7. Jenny Creighton			
8. Eb Carron			

Name _____

Keeping Track of Events

Read each chapter below, and answer the question about that chapter on the lines provided. If you need more room to write, use the other side of this page, or use a separate sheet of paper.

CHAPTER 4   **At Shad's**—*When Jethro goes to visit Shad, he wants to know whether Bill was right in his thinking about war.*

What does he learn from Shad?

_____

_____

CHAPTER 5   **In the woods**—*Jethro survives a moment of grave danger in a surprising way.*

What happens to bring Jethro home safely?

_____

_____

CHAPTER 6   **At home**—*After Jethro's narrow escape, two things happen that threaten the Creightons' survival.*

What are those two events?

_____

_____

CHAPTER 7   **The war comes home**—*Jenny says that she didn't know what war was till Dan Lawrence brought "this awful word."*

What does she mean?

_____

_____

CHAPTER 7   **In town**—*Guy Wortman finally gets his "comeuppance."*

What happens to him?

_____

_____

Making Inferences

Read each chapter listed below; then answer the question about that chapter. If you need more room to write, use the other side of this page, or use a separate sheet of paper.

CHAPTER 8   *Despite their belief in their cause, Americans from both sides begin to desert.*

What is wearing away their commitment?

_____

_____

CHAPTER 9   *Jethro finds that Eb has deserted and decides to shelter him and write to the President.*

Why does this decision worry Jethro so much?

_____

_____

CHAPTER 10   *Matt Creighton decides to allow Jenny to marry Shad.*

What convinces Matt to change his mind?

_____

_____

CHAPTER 11   *After Lincoln's Proclamation of Amnesty, Matt Creighton says, "Never hev I loved him so much."*

How does this fit with what Mr. Creighton has said and done before?

_____

_____

CHAPTER 12   *Ross Milton warns Jethro, "Don't expect peace to be a perfect pearl."*

What does the editor mean by this statement?

_____

_____

Literary Concept 1

THEME

The theme of a literary work is an insight about life or human nature that the writer presents to the reader. In *Across Five Aprils* Irene Hunt offers some of her ideas about inflexible beliefs, about war, about hardship. Below are several thematic statements. Make notes to show how each idea is shown in the novel. Then give another example from real life based on your own experience or events you've heard or read about. You might work with another student or in small groups.

1. Individual loyalties can conflict with the values and loyalties of a community.

How shown in novel:

_____

Real life example:

_____

2. Most often there are no real winners in a war; both sides suffer.

How shown in novel:

_____

Real life example:

_____

3. Some decisions in life are difficult because they are not clearly right or wrong.

How shown in novel:

_____

Real life example:

_____

4. Our lives are affected by circumstances beyond our control.

How shown in novel:

_____

Real life example:

_____

5. Hardship and the challenge to one's beliefs offer the opportunity for growth.

How shown in novel:

_____

Real life example:

_____

6. Justice does not always proceed according to human timetables or individual ideas of right and wrong.

How shown in novel:

_____

Real life example:

_____

Name _____

In many novels, the central character goes through great changes in attitude and understanding. The changes are often shown in the character's own words and actions, or in comments about the character made by other characters or by the narrator. To show these changes in Jethro, fill out the chart below as you read *Across Five Aprils.*

- The first column contains something said by or about Jethro and the chapter and page number in which the quote appears.

- In the second column, identify who made the statement.

- In the third column, write how and why Jethro has changed at this point, as in the example.

Statement	Speaker	How Jethro has changed
1. Suddenly he was deeply troubled. He groped toward an understanding of something that was far beyond the excitement of guns and shouting men (Chapter 2, p. 00)	Narrator	Jethro is beginning to understand the terrible, complex reality of war.
2. He no longer talked to the children, though; a phase of innocence had passed, which would never be recaptured. (Chapter 3, p. 00)		
3. *You tell Jethro that bein a soljer ain't so much.* (Chapter 4, p. 00)		
4. If someone had asked Jethro to name a time when he left childhood behind him, he might have named that last week of March in 1862. (Chapter 6, p. 00)		
5. Jethro nodded. "I allow to get thanks—" he paused and flushed as he looked up at the editor. "I want to send thanks to him—one way or the other." (Chapter 8, p. 00)		
6. "If I could be sure I'm doin' the right thing," he would say to himself, as he watched the dark earth fall away from his plowshares. "If I could feel really set-up about doin' a fine thing, but I don't know. Maybe I'm doin' somethin' terrible wrong; maybe the next time they come, the Federal Registrars will take me." (Chapter 9, p. 00)		
7. But on the last Sunday of that April, a Sunday of sunlight and bright sky, Jethro lay in the grass on Walnut Hill, and rage mingled with grief in his heart. (Chapter 12, p. 00)		

Beyond the Literature
SYNTHESIZING IDEAS

Culminating Writing Assignments

EXPLORATORY WRITING

1. The last words of *Across Five Aprils* are "…all the shadows were lifted from the April morning." Think about the last two chapters and this ending. Write an **essay** about the ending of the novel, telling whether you thought it was a happy ending, a sad ending, or something else.

2. The last word from Bill is in John's letter from Nashville, after his visit with his brother among the Confederate prisoners. Think about Bill's position and choices throughout *Across Five Aprils*, and write a **letter** from him to Jethro, dated the day the terms of peace are signed at Appomattox Court House.

RESEARCH

1. In Chapter 12, Irene Hunt describes how people in Illinois reacted to Sherman's march of destruction. Research this episode of the Civil War, and then write a **newspaper editorial** about whether the destruction was justified or not.

2. In Chapter 11, Shadrach Yale writes that he has revised his opinion of his former commander, General McClellan. Research biographical data about McClellan, finding at least two different authors' views of him. Then write a **journal entry** by General McClellan assessing his strengths and weaknesses in war and peace.

LITERARY ANALYSIS

1. Choose one of the following themes:
   - Individual loyalties can conflict with the values and loyalties of a community.
   - Our lives are often affected by circumstances beyond our control.
   - Some decisions are difficult to make because they are neither wrong nor right.

   Then choose one of the characters in the novel—Jethro, Bill, Shad, Matt Creighton or Jenny Creighton—and write a **critical essay** explaining how his or her experiences illustrate or contradict the theme.

2. Write a **character sketch** about Jethro in *Across Five Aprils*. Show how Jethro changes from the beginning of the novel to its end, emphasizing the episodes that contribute most to Jethro's growth.

3. Write a **comparison** between *Across Five Aprils* and one of the related readings, such as "The Drummer Boy of Shiloh" or "The Sniper." Compare the two works on the basis of several elements such as character, theme, setting, or mood.

   For writing instruction in specific modes, have students use the Writing Coach in the **CommonSpace** program.

Multimodal Activities

Map Maker

Have students turn to Chapter 4, where Shad draws a map to illustrate for Jethro the importance of the western campaign. Ask students to make their own **map,** based on what Shad says and on what they can find in their history books on the Civil War. Students can compare their efforts when done.

Ballad of the Burdows

The Burdows were a family so despised they were nicknamed the "Jail Burdows." The name seems deserved when Travis Burdow's drunken prank ends in Mary Creighton's death. Dave Burdow, however, redeems the family's reputation. Have students write a **folk ballad** about the Burdows—a family that seems destined for jail but confounds fate in the end.

Guy's Comeuppance

Guy Wortman finally gets his "comeuppance" in a very satisfying way. Have students draw a **cartoon** of the scene in which this takes place. Display these cartoons in class. If they prefer, students may make cartoons of something else from the novel, such as a "copperhead."

Eb on Trial

Imagine that Eb Carron is tracked down after the war and brought to trial by zealous army officers wishing to make an example of him. Have students stage a **trial** for him, with a defense lawyer, a prosecutor, a judge, and witnesses, both from the novel and from Eb's army unit. The class can serve as jury, determining whether Eb should be punished, and what his punishment should be. Jethro may also be indicted.

Across Five Aprils, the Movie

Have students make plans for a movie version of the novel. They should pick a cast, using current actors. They should then decide what scenes to dramatize, how to convey the feel of war, and so on. They can devise **storyboards** for the important scenes they choose, and present some to the class. When done, students might like to see what one film of this novel looks like—see Additional Resources, pages 45–47.

From the Battlefield

A group of students can imagine that modern communications are available to interview soldiers in a Civil War battle. They may conduct an **interview** with one of the characters in the novel in an actual battle, having him describe what it's like. Students taking the parts of officers, settlers, nurses, women dressed as men so they can fight, may also be interviewed. This skit can be videotaped or put on "live" for the class.

Model Battle

Have students investigate one Civil War battle, for example, the battle of Shiloh, and make a **model** showing how the battle developed, and where Tom died. They may use toy soldiers or cardboard models to represent troops, formations, attacks, defenses, and so on. The model can be displayed and "activated" during a class.

War Games

Encourage students to play the computer-simulation **games** of the American Civil War that are widely available. Board games based on specific battles are also available in hobby shops.

Cross-Curricular Projects

Coming of Age

Overview:

In this project, students will examine how the conceptions of growing up differ from culture to culture and from one generation to another. Their task is to investigate the different ways of growing up.

Cross-Curricular Connection: Social Studies

Suggested Procedure:

1. Explain to students that they will be investigating the various meanings that "growing up," or "coming of age," had at various times, and in various cultures. They might identify examples of these meanings in *Across Five Aprils.* Their task is to gather additional meanings. Some cultures have specific ages at which a person is considered "grown up," while others do not; some have specific rituals that mark the passage into the role of "grown-up," while others do not. Students individually and in groups will investigate some of these practices, and then report to the class as a whole.

2. Once students understand what they are looking for, have them explore what "growing up" means to them and their classmates. Help them see that even within their own peer group the concept has various meanings that may change according to conditions such as:

   • chronological age

   • physical size

   • general political and social circumstances, including war

   • cultural expectations (including religious beliefs and values)

   These variations can come out in discussion because students are from different backgrounds, and so will already have different ideas about what "growing up" means. If any students or groups wish to investigate a culture other than their own, encourage them to do so. Students may benefit from choosing how to gather and present information using interviews, surveys, graphs, or charts, for example, to record the various meanings of "growing up," and the conditions that affect those meanings.

3. Have students prepare a simple questionnaire, with a dozen or so specific questions to ask parents and/or grandparents about *their* growing up. Students should ask their respondents if there was a particular age at which they were considered grown up; if there were associated rituals, either official or unofficial; what responsibilities being "grown up" entailed, what growing up meant to them, and so on.

4. Set aside class time for students and groups to report their findings.

Teaching Tip

If time is a problem, have the class do only the in-class part of the project, discussing the ideas and information they already have on the subject. Encourage those who wish to write further on the subject for extra credit to do so.

Songs and War

Overview:

In Chapter 12 of *Across Five Aprils,* Irene Hunt writes of the end-of-war celebration in which thousands sang "The Battle Hymn of the Republic." In this project, groups of students will investigate both Civil War songs and songs that have come to be associated with other American wars. Groups will be asked to research, report on, and perform or play record- ings of songs from different wars. By using various media, they can make the project as complex as you wish.

Cross-Curricular Connections: Music, Film, Theater, History

Suggested Procedure:

1. Remind students of the two most famous Civil War songs, "The Battle Hymn of the Republic" and "Dixie." Explain that other wars also have songs associated with them, and that they will be working in groups to investigate them.

2. Divide the students into groups, each group to research a different war and the songs associated with it; some examples are the Revolutionary War, the War of 1812, the Civil War, World War I, World War II, the Vietnam War. Each group will be responsible for finding at least one song associated with that war, getting the words and music to it, find- ing out something about its composer and composition, and why it became emblematic of that war. They may enlist parents, music teach- ers, librarians, music stores, and others in the project.

3. Each group will present its findings. They may display sheet music on poster board or show videos of old films. The presentation must also include some history of the song(s), and a performance of the song(s), preferably by the students themselves.

4. As a conclusion, students can discuss why wars tend to have songs written for them, or associated with them. How does the spirit of song relate to the martial spirit, or other feelings people have about war?

Teaching Tip

For Your Information: see Additional Resources, pages 45–47, for a full citation of *The Spirit of the Sixties: A History of the Civil War in Song.*

A Civil War Homefront Exhibit

Overview:

The aim of this project is to collect information and memorabilia, if available, about the way the Civil War affected the students' particular town, county, state, or region. The materials can be displayed in a class exhibit to be shared with others in the school.

Cross-Curricular Connections: History, Art, Science

Suggested Procedure:

1. Explain to the students that they will be creating a small Civil War museum in their classroom to show memorabilia, taped or videotaped remembrances, and news stories from their own area. They will be doing something similar to what Irene Hunt does in *Across Five Aprils,* that is, to focus on how the war affected people not directly involved in the fighting. They may also use items that recall the Civil War, such as the fabrics that were used for dressing wounds, or foods.

2. Divide students into groups, each of which will research a different aspect of the homefront, for example, local opinion about the war; local photographs from the period of the war and of local war-related activities; information on local and state fighting units such as regiments or battalions; local initiatives supporting the troops in battle; news articles and/or editorials about the war; the importance of the terrain in nearby battle sites; shortages and other economic effects; dissent; and so on. Point out that the local library and the local newspaper are invaluable resources for this project. Each group will compare and contrast their findings with the effects of the Civil War on Jasper County, Illinois, as the narrator of *Across Five Aprils* describes them.

3. Each group will be responsible for research and for a neat and pleasing presentation of the information, accompanied by a spoken account. Help student groups organize themselves. Set aside classroom time for the whole class to identify problems, brainstorm solutions, and share resources.

4. Set aside classroom time for each group to make its presentation and answer any questions.

Teaching Tip

If time is short, limit the project to research and a simple in-class presentation by each group.

Suggestions for Assessment

Negotiated Rubrics

Negotiating rubrics for assessment with students allows them to know before they start an assignment what is required and how it will be judged, and gives them additional ownership of the final product. A popular method of negotiating rubrics is for the teacher and students respectively to list the qualities that the final product should contain, then compare the teacher-generated list with the student-generated list and together decide on a compromise.

Portfolio Building

Remind students that they have many choices of types of assignments to select for their portfolios. Among these are the following:

- Culminating Writing Assignments on page 36
- Writing Prompts, found in the Discussion Starters
- Multimodal Activities (pages 37–38)
- Cross-Curricular Projects (pages 39–41)

Suggest that students use some of the following questions as criteria in selecting which pieces to include in their portfolios.

- Which shows my clearest thinking about the literature?
- Which is or could become most complete?
- Which shows a type of work not presently included in my portfolio?
- Which am I proudest of?

Remind students to reflect on the pieces they choose and to attach a note explaining why they included each and how they would evaluate it.

*For suggestions on how to assess portfolios, see **Portfolio Building** in the **Testing and Assessment** booklet.*

Writing Assessment

The following can be made into formal assignments for evaluation:

- Culminating Writing Assignments on page 35
- a written analysis of the Critic's Corner literary criticism
- fully developed Writing Prompts from the Discussion Starters

*For suggestions about assessing specific kinds of writing, see **Writing Guidelines and Rubrics** in the **Testing and Assessment** booklet.*

Alternative Assessment

The following can be used for performance and product assessment.

- Multimodal Activities on pages 37–38
- Cross-Curricular Projects on pages 39–41

Test

The test on page 43 comprises an essay and short-answer questions. The answer key follows.

Test

Across Five Aprils and Related Readings

Essay

Choose two of the following essay questions to answer on your own paper.
(25 points each)

1. Irene Hunt uses her title, *Across Five Aprils,* to give form to her novel. Explain how she does this. Consider a) what the title actually refers to; b) connotations associated with the month of April; c) the way at least one character's associations with the month of April are related to the war.

2. In Chapter 1, Ellen Creighton says, "He's like a man standin' where two roads meet, Jethro…and one road is as dark and fearsome as the other; there ain't a choice between the two, and yet a choice has to be made." Her simile about the President also expresses one of the themes of the novel as a whole. Explain some of the ways this is so. You may include the choices made by President Lincoln, Jethro, Jenny, Bill, or others.

3. Choose one of the following pairs to compare and contrast:

   a. Jethro and the drummer boy in "The Drummer Boy of Shiloh"

   b. Bill and the sniper in "The Sniper"

   c. Guy Wortman and the sniper in "The Sniper"

   Consider how each person handles what life has called on him to do.

4. Several people in *Across Five Aprils* make decisions that violate either popular opinion or the law. Matt Creighton, Bill Creighton, and Jethro all do this. Choose one whose decision you think required the most courage, explaining your choice. Write whether you agree with that person's decision, and why or why not.

Short Answer

On your paper, write a short answer for each question below and give a reason for your answer. (5 points each)

1. Discuss at least one way in which Jethro changes between the first and fourth April.

2. Why is Bill's leaving so important?

3. Why do you think Dave Burdow helps Jethro get home safely?

4. What does the label "Copperhead" have to do with the Creightons?

5. Choose one of the Creightons and describe his or her attitude toward the war in the opening pages and how it changes as time goes on.

6. How does Jenny's refusal to share Shad's letter affect Jethro?

7. How does Tom's death change the war for Jenny and Jethro?

8. What worries Ed Turner most about his son's letter describing Sherman's march through Georgia?

9. How would you describe Jethro's attitude toward deserters?

10. How is Jethro affected by President Lincoln's death?

Test Answer Key

Answers to essay questions will vary, but opinions should be stated clearly and supported by details from the novel. Suggestions for points to look for are given below.

1. The novel is organized "across five Aprils," from 1861 to 1865, the years during which the Civil War took place. Each April marks a different stage in people's perception of the war: from optimism to disillusion to despair. The fifth April, at first a joyous one because of the end of the war, becomes with Lincoln's death the "saddest and most cruel of the five." This irony—of April, the month of spring growth that becomes, with the war, the month of death—pervades and structures the novel. Jethro's expectations about the month of April are consistently undermined by the events of the war.

2. Ellen's words illustrate the theme "Some decisions are difficult to make because they are neither wrong nor right." Several characters are faced with such choices as is the country as a whole when it chooses war. Lincoln has to choose between allowing the country to be split in half or declaring a war in which so many can be killed. Jethro must make such a choice when he chooses to disobey the law against harboring deserters in order to save his cousin Eb. Bill has to make such a choice when he joins the Confederate army knowing he is opposing his own family and may face his own brothers on a battlefield. Matt earlier has made such a choice in averting vengeance; he makes another when he allows Jenny to go to Washington to see and marry Shad.

3. a. Jethro and the drummer boy are both young and naive about war. Both learn from authority figures how to behave under stress: Shad and Ross Milton in Jethro's case, the general in the other case. The general's advice to the drummer boy could well be lethal; what Shad and Ross teach Jethro is quite different—to be flexible in belief, and not to rush to judgment.

   b. Both Bill and the sniper enter situations where they are at war with their brothers. Bill is not a "fanatic," however. Nor does the sniper appear to be someone who would write a letter assuring his mother that he did not, or would not, kill his brother.

   c. Guy Wortman and the sniper resemble each other in that both are zealots. The sniper even shoots an old woman; Guy Wortman would have injured or killed Jethro, and destroys a whole family's living. The sniper, however, shows courage in battle against equals; Wortman shows cowardice by staying home and attacking children and defenseless families.

4. Opinions will vary because all three made decisions requiring courage: Matt stood up to his community when he defied the code of revenge; Bill went against his family's and community's loyalty to the Union; Jethro violated the law concerning deserters. Shad says that Bill's decision required the most courage of all—precisely because it violated popular opinion and was based on his own reasoning about right and wrong. Students may say that Jethro's decision was the most difficult because it was made by a young person without influence risking himself on behalf of another. Jethro's decision is a high point for him in the novel.

Short Answer

Answers will vary but should reflect the following ideas:

1. Jethro takes initiative by doing something illegal when he helps Eb; he is a little "forward" by writing a letter to President Lincoln; he is conscious of his responsibility to his family as the only son who remains at home.

2. Bill is Jethro's favorite brother; the war now becomes literally brother against brother; Bill has gone against family and community, thus putting the family in trouble with the community.

3. To pay back Matt Creighton for saving his own son from hanging; because he is a better man than others consider him to be.

4. The word means "Southern sympathizer" and is applied to the family when Bill joins the Confederate army. It results in the attack on Jethro and the barn-burning.

5. Guy Wortman and his crew of nightriders are opposed to "Copperheads"; they are terrorists, attempting to silence those who disagree with them.

6. It creates a distance between Jenny and Jethro because she is growing up and away from her family; it shows an intimacy between Shad and Jenny that Jethro can't share.

7. It brings the war home, making Jethro realize that those who die are not always distant strangers; it makes the war personally tragic rather than remote and romantic.

8. Turner worries about the effect of so much killing on his son's morals.

9. Jethro is ambivalent: he disapproves of people running away, but sympathizes with the fear he sees in Eb's face; Eb is a real, familiar person, not an abstract principle.

10. Because of the letter he receives, Jethro sees Lincoln as a personal friend; he admires Lincoln very much and realizes that the country is now leaderless.

Additional Resources

Other Works by Irene Hunt

Up a Road Slowly. Chicago: Follett, 1966.
At the age of seven, Julie Trilling goes to live with her aunt after the death of her mother. The book covers ten years of Julie's life, during which she develops from a tantrum-throwing child to a gracious young woman.

Trial of Apple Blossoms. Chicago: Follett, 1968.
A portrait of Jonathan Chapman, "Johnny Appleseed," who explains his philosophy about the war, bigotry, injustice, and love for all living things.

No Promise in the Wind. Chicago: Follett, 1970.
A fifteen-year-old boy struggles to survive and to resolve his inner conflicts during the Great Depression.

The Lottery Rose. New York: Scribner's, 1976.
A young victim of child abuse gradually overcomes fear and suspicions when he is placed in a home with other boys.

William. New York: Scribner's, 1977.
Three orphaned black children form a new and loving family group with a white teen-age girl.

Claws of a Young Century. New York: Scribner's, 1980.
Seventeen-year-old Ellen's optimistic dream of a bright new century on New Year's Eve, 1899, seems a far cry from the reality of her next twenty years fighting the battles for women's suffrage.

The Everlasting Hills. New York: Scribner's, 1985.
When a bitter mountain man cannot accept his twelve-year-old son's mental retardation, the boy wanders into the wilderness to find in a stranger the family love he never had.

FICTION

Crane, Stephen. *The Red Badge of Courage.* New York: Viking, 1984. The timeless story of a boy who joins the Union army and finds out in his first battle—the Battle of Chancellorsville in 1863—that courage is made of different stuff than he had imagined. **(challenge)**

Rhodes, James A. *Johnny Shiloh: A Novel of the Civil War.* Indianapolis: Bobbs-Merrill, 1959. The story of Johnny Clem, an actual drummer boy who joined the Union army at twelve and became a non-commissioned officer by the time he was fourteen. **(average)**

Walker, Margaret. *Jubilee.* Boston: Houghton-Mifflin, 1966. Walker details the joys and hardships of Vyry Brown and her African-American family in Georgia during and after the Civil War. They find that freedom does not come because governments decree it, nor do human attitudes and behaviors change because of new laws. **(challenge)**

NONFICTION

Catton, Bruce. *This Hallowed Ground: The Story of the Union Side in the Civil War.* Garden City, NY: Doubleday, 1956. The pre-eminent historian of the Civil War tells the story in an illustrated edition for younger readers. **(easy)**

Chang, Ina. *A Separate Battle: Women and the Civil War.* New York: Lodestar Books, 1991. Ina Chang focuses on the little-known roles women played as soldiers and nurses, and on the homefront during the Civil War. **(average)**

Cox, Clinton. *Undying Glory: The Story of the Massachusetts 54th Regiment.* New York: Scholastic Hardcover, 1991. Clinton Cox tells the story, recently filmed by Hollywood, of the first African-American regiment to fight in the Civil War. **(average)**

Freedman, Russell. *Lincoln: A Photobiography.* New York: Ticknor & Fields, 1987. Russell Freedman's biography is liberally laced with photographs and prints. Tracing Lincoln's early life, it focuses on the Civil War years up to and including the President's death and includes samples of Lincoln's most important writings. **(easy)**

Glass, Paul. *The Spirit of the Sixties: A History of the Civil War in Song.* St. Louis: Educational Publishers, 1964. Glass's book gives fascinating details about the history and origins of famous and not-so-famous songs from the Civil War period, including "The Battle Hymn of the Republic," and "Dixie." A music score is included for each song. **(average)**

Kantor, MacKinlay. *Gettysburg.* New York: Random House, 1987. The renowned Civil War historian describes both the battle and its impact on the people in that part of Pennsylvania. **(easy)**

Meltzer, Milton, ed. *Voices from the Civil War: A Documentary History of the Great American Conflict.* New York: HarperCollins, 1989. Milton Meltzer collected letters, diaries, ballads, newspaper interviews, speeches, and memoirs from those who participated in the Civil War. Among those excerpted are Frederick Douglass, John Brown, Henry David Thoreau, Mark Twain, and Walt Whitman. **(average)**

Piggins, Carol Ann. *A Multicultural Portrait of the Civil War.* New York: Marshall Cavendish, 1994. This book focuses on the Civil War's effect on the marginal people: Native Americans, women both at home and at the front, slaves and runaways, Irish immigrants, and Quakers. **(easy)**

Taylor, Susie King. *A Black Woman's Civil War Memoirs: Reminiscences of My Life in Camp with the 33rd U.S. Colored Troops, Late 1st South Carolina Volunteers.* New York: M. Weiner, 1988. A reprint of the memoirs of an African-American woman who saw the Civil War from ground level. **(challenge)**

Whitman, Walt. *Walt Whitman's Civil War.* Ed. Walter Lowenfels. New York: Alfred Knopf, 1960. The great poet's prose writings on the war include his eyewitness accounts of Civil War battlefields, hospitals, and the streets of Washington, D.C., in both victory and defeat. **(challenge)**

MULTIMEDIA

Across Five Aprils. Deerfield, IL: Learning Corporation of America, 1990. Hunt's novel of the Civil War as seen from the homefront is produced in two parts: Part 1: A Time to Choose, and Part 2: War and Hope. 2 cassettes, 67 min. **(videocassette)**

The Birth of a Nation. Los Angeles, CA: Republic Pictures Home Video [1991], c. 1915. Produced and directed by D.W. Griffiths. One of the pioneer silent films, this 1915 spectacular depicts both the Civil War and the ensuing conflicts of Reconstruction in the South, including the birth of the Ku Klux Klan. 1 cassette, 154 min. **(videocassette)**

The Civil War. Alexandria, VA: PBS Video, 1990. The by-now classic Ken Burns documentary of the Civil War as told through interviews, documents, photographs, letters, and diary entries. 9 cassettes, 680 min. **(videocassette)**

Glory. Burbank, CA: RCA/Columbia Pictures Home Video, 1990. Produced by Pieter Jan Brugge. This film of the black 54th Massachusetts Infantry Regiment features Matthew Broderick, Denzel Washington, and Morgan Freeman. 1 cassette. 122 min. **(videocassette)**

The Massachusetts 54th Colored Infantry. Alexandria, VA: PBS Video, 1991. Produced by Jacqueline Shearer. This PBS documentary tells the story of the first officially sanctioned regiment of northern black soldiers formed in Boston during the Civil War. 1 cassette, 58 min. **(videocassette)**

The Red Badge of Courage. Charlotte Hall, MD: Recorded Books, 1981. A sound recording of the full text of Stephen Crane's novel, as read by Frank Muller. 3 cassettes, 270 min. **(audiocassette)**